I0446768

# Jesus Christ

## The Greatest CEO of All Time

The True Measure of a Leader Is Not in His Title, but in His Sacrifice.

Paulo Ehms

MMXXIII

For permission requests, please contact:
ehmsbooks@yahoo.com

# Table of Content

# Jesus Christ

# The Greatest CEO of All Time

In the contemporary business world, the figure of the CEO is emblematic of success and effective leadership. CEOs are visionaries, strategists, and, above all, managers who inspire action, innovation, and loyalty. But what if we looked back at one of history's most influential leaders and considered him in the same light? This book proposes to do exactly that, analyzing the life and teachings of Jesus Christ through the lens of modern business management.

The idea of Jesus as a CEO might seem anachronistic or even irreverent at first glance. However, by considering the fundamentals of leadership—establishing a vision, building teams, inspiring trust, innovating, and overcoming adversity—we find remarkable parallels between biblical teachings and contemporary leadership practices. Jesus not only founded an organization—the Church—that has endured for more than two millennia, but also demonstrated leadership principles that transcend time and cultural context.

This book is neither a theological dissertation nor a dogmatic business manual. Instead, it explores how events and parables from the life of Jesus resemble the journey and challenges of a modern CEO. From recruiting the Twelve Apostles—his "executive team"—to crisis management and establishing a lasting legacy, the biblical narrative provides fertile ground for leadership lessons.

Through this book, entrepreneurs, managers, and leaders will gain a fresh perspective on everyday challenges. By adapting Jesus's strategies to modern business, we can discover innovative approaches to leadership that promote positive impact, sustainability, and a sense of mission that goes beyond profits and metrics.

Therefore, I invite you to open your mind and explore with me the potential applications of Jesus's teachings in today's business environment. Together, let's uncover how the greatest leader in history could very well be considered the greatest CEO of all time.

# Chapter 1

## Vision and Mission

## The Foundation of Transformational Leadership

In this chapter, we delve deeply into the essence of leadership exemplified by Jesus Christ, observing how he established a vision and mission that continue to resonate powerfully and relevantly more than two millennia later. By carefully analyzing Jesus' methods and communication, it becomes possible to understand how he created a solid foundation that drove historical movements and significant social transformations. This same principle of a solid and well-articulated foundation is essential for contemporary CEOs, who must clearly define and effectively communicate their organizational visions and missions, guiding their teams through the complex challenges of the modern corporate world.

## The Transformational Vision of Jesus

By closely examining the 'Sermon on the Mount', we discover not just a spiritual discourse but a detailed manifesto that clearly outlined a powerful and compelling vision of an ideal future. Additionally, it established a profound set of human and spiritual values, which in many ways resembles a contemporary corporate mission statement. This sermon was crucial because it managed to inspire and unite diverse individuals around a common cause—something historical leaders like Martin Luther King Jr. and innovative CEOs like Steve Jobs successfully achieved, driving profound changes and continuous innovation.

Jesus did not merely speak about a utopian vision but demonstrated its meaning through concrete life actions, exemplifying leadership by example—a crucial principle for contemporary business leaders aiming to build trust and cohesion within their teams.

## The 'Sermon on the Mount' as a Corporate Mission

A particularly fascinating aspect of the 'Sermon on the Mount' is the Beatitudes, presenting values such as mercy, justice, purity of heart, and peacemaking. When transposed into the contemporary business context, these values equate to a vigorous advocacy for business ethics, social responsibility, and commitment to human and environmental well-being. Modern companies like Patagonia, known for environmental commitment, and Google, which emphasizes ethical innovation, clearly illustrate how a mission driven by authentic values can define business strategies, positively influence daily operations, and foster loyalty among employees and customers.

Moreover, commitment to these values can create a strong corporate identity differentiated within today's highly competitive market, promoting a positive public image and deep emotional connections with consumers.

## The Parable of the Talents and the Importance of Vision in Leadership

The well-known parable of the talents clearly highlights the importance of effective resource management and the necessity for constant growth and innovation, perfectly reflecting the challenges faced by modern CEOs. A notable example is Anne Mulcahy, former CEO of Xerox, who radically realigned the company's vision and mission, avoiding imminent bankruptcy and restoring its position in the global market. The practical application of this parable in the contemporary corporate world is also corroborated by modern theories on leadership and motivation, such as those proposed by Daniel Pink, emphasizing intrinsic motivation and clearly defined purpose as foundations for superior, sustainable performance.

Therefore, by applying this biblical teaching, business leaders are encouraged to promote not just economic efficiency but also an organizational culture centered on personal and collective growth.

## Implications of Jesus' Vision and Mission for Modern CEOs

Transposing the teachings and visionary approach of Jesus Christ into today's business context offers a powerful and practical perspective on transformational leadership. Simon Sinek, one of today's most influential thinkers on leadership, asserts that effective leaders should always "Start with Why," highlighting the critical importance of a central mission that inspires and mobilizes teams and stakeholders. Such perspective profoundly echoes the clarity of purpose Jesus demonstrated in his leadership—an element equally essential for historical leaders such as Winston Churchill, especially during crises.

These implications clearly demonstrate that clarity, effective communication, and coherence between actions and values are absolutely fundamental for any contemporary leader seeking lasting success.

We conclude this chapter by synthesizing how the vision and mission exemplified by Jesus Christ transcend strictly religious boundaries, constituting universal principles of timeless leadership highly applicable to today's business world. Furthermore, we highlight that the ethics and philosophy underlying these concepts resonate with historical philosophical ideas from influential thinkers like Aristotle and Immanuel Kant, suggesting effective business management goes beyond generating immediate profit. It fundamentally involves inspiring people, leading with integrity, and promoting a higher purpose transcending purely financial goals.

This chapter represents merely the beginning of a profound and transformative journey that seeks to explore how Jesus' principles and teachings can shed light on modern leadership practices. CEOs and business leaders adopting these principles can guide their organizations toward economic success while positively transforming the lives of the people around them.

# The Sermon on the Mount

## Wisdom for Modern Times

Today, more than ever, we face challenges that demand profound wisdom, clarity of purpose, and the courage to act with justice and compassion. If Jesus Christ were standing before us right now, perhaps his words would sound like this:

**Blessed are the humble, for they shall lead with integrity and compassion, and their actions will build bridges in a divided world.**

**Blessed are those who feel the pain of the world and seek justice, for they shall become agents of change and inspiration to many.**

**Happy are the humble, those who know how to listen and value others, for they will create strong and united communities.**

**Happy are those who thirst for justice and equality, for they shall build fairer and more sustainable societies.**

**Blessed are those who practice mercy and forgiveness, for they shall be living examples of peace and reconciliation.**

**Blessed are those whose hearts are pure and honest, for they will clearly see paths toward genuine solutions.**

**Happy are those who promote peace, for they will be recognized as true leaders and social transformers.**

**Strong and blessed are those who remain faithful to their values, even when criticized, for they shall build lasting legacies.**

You are like lights in an often dark world. Do not hide your brightness; inspire through example, act with compassion, and become living models of the values you proclaim.

## On Judgment and Empathy

Do not judge hastily, but strive to understand, listen, and learn before pointing out faults. Understand that with the same rigor you evaluate others, you will also be evaluated.

Do unto others exactly as you would have them do unto you; this is the fundamental basis of any healthy and sustainable relationship, personal or professional.

## On Priorities and Anxieties

Do not live trapped by anxiety about tomorrow, for each day has its own battles. Focus on the essentials, on values that are eternal. Life is more valuable than mere material accumulation, and true wealth lies in relationships and purpose.

Observe the nature around you: if God cares so deeply for it, how much more will He care for you, who are immensely valuable in His eyes? Trust this and live with gratitude.

## On Resilience and Solid Foundations

Those who hear these words and put them into practice are like someone who builds their house upon a solid and secure foundation. When storms, challenges, and difficulties come, their life remains firm and intact, for it is grounded in solid and true principles.

On the other hand, those who hear but do not act coherently are like someone who builds upon unstable sand; when problems arise, their structure quickly collapses.

## On Authenticity and Consistency

Be coherent in all that you do, living your beliefs and ideals in every action and decision. An authentic life is not measured by words but by the consistency of your actions and the positive impact you leave on the lives of others.

Today, more than ever, we need leaders who embody these timeless truths. Leaders who have the courage to love and serve, who face adversity with calm and clarity, and who cultivate a lasting legacy through empathy, innovation, and commitment to the common good.

By following this path, you will not only transform your lives and organizations but also create a fairer, more compassionate, and sustainable society. This is the true legacy that endures, and this is the leadership that truly transforms the world.

# Chapter 2

## Building a Team

## Jesus's Recruitment and Diversity Strategies

The success of any organization depends heavily on the strength, cohesion, and diversity of its team. Jesus profoundly understood this reality and carefully chose his disciples, each with distinct skills, backgrounds, and personalities, to form a group that would transcend generations and deeply impact humanity. In this chapter, we will thoroughly examine how Jesus identified, recruited, developed, and managed his followers, exploring valuable lessons these methods provide for building highly effective teams in modern management.

## Selection of the Twelve Apostles: Recruitment Strategies

When selecting his disciples, Jesus did not follow traditional recruitment criteria emphasizing only technical or social qualifications. Instead, he chose individuals with diverse backgrounds and characteristics, including simple fishermen like Peter, Andrew, James, and John; a tax collector, Matthew, who was poorly viewed by society; and Simon the Zealot, a fervent political activist. This unconventional approach highlights his ability to identify human potential where others saw limitations. Contemporary business leaders adopt similar strategies when recruiting people with unique skills or experiences that don't necessarily fit traditional profiles. Clear examples include companies like Google and Tesla, which often hire professionals from diverse disciplines, creating creative and innovative teams.

## Diversity and Inclusion: Jesus's Team

Diversity was a fundamental characteristic of the group formed by Jesus. His team brought together people from different social classes, mentalities, and professions, which was highly innovative for the time. Contemporary research shows diverse teams are more creative, innovative, and resilient, a reality confirmed by studies from institutions such as IBM and McKinsey & Company. These studies affirm that companies cultivating diversity in gender, ethnicity, culture, and experience are significantly more successful financially and operationally. Jesus anticipated this concept by bringing together a heterogeneous group that, despite their differences, shared a clear common objective. Current business leaders, such as Apple's Tim Cook and Facebook's Sheryl Sandberg, continually emphasize the importance of inclusion and diversity as pillars for organizational sustainability and success.

## Managing Diverse Personalities

Jesus demonstrated exceptional skill in managing the diversity of personalities and temperaments within his team. He effectively navigated Peter's impulsiveness and enthusiasm, Thomas's introspection and skepticism, and directly addressed the challenge of Judas's betrayal. These examples provide valuable lessons on the importance of emotional intelligence, empathy, and adaptability in modern leadership. Contemporary CEOs like Satya Nadella from Microsoft consistently highlight the importance of cultivating empathy, self-awareness, and understanding to successfully lead diverse teams. Modern companies invest significantly in emotional intelligence training and interpersonal skills precisely to replicate this effective management of human differences.

## Empowerment and Delegation of Authority

Jesus not only selected a diverse team but also empowered his disciples through significant delegation of authority. By sending the disciples out independently to preach and perform miracles, he demonstrated complete trust in their individual and collective capabilities. This practice aligns with modern organizational empowerment principles, where employees are given sufficient autonomy to make important decisions and implement innovative ideas. CEOs like Mary Barra of General Motors and Reed Hastings of Netflix actively advocate delegation as a vital means to stimulate innovation, increase motivation, and ensure organizational agility in highly competitive corporate environments.

## Team Culture and Conflict Resolution

Conflicts are inevitable in any human group, and Jesus's team was no exception. Several biblical passages document disagreements among his followers, whether due to the pursuit of recognition, ideological disagreements, or communication failures. Nevertheless, Jesus consistently promoted a culture of openness, dialogue, and forgiveness, showing that conflicts are not insurmountable problems but opportunities for growth. Modern conflict resolution models, such as the one developed by Kenneth Thomas and Ralph Kilmann, underline the effectiveness of the empathetic and dialogical approach Jesus used, teaching business leaders how to create healthy environments where conflicts are positively managed and leveraged for organizational development.

## Investing in Continuous Development

Jesus continuously invested in his team's development through teachings, reflections, and ongoing feedback. He created an environment where disciples could continuously learn and grow, an essential element of modern talent management practices. Companies such as Microsoft, Google, and Amazon strongly emphasize the continuous development and professional empowerment of their teams, providing constant learning opportunities, training, and regular feedback—practices already adopted by Jesus in his daily leadership.

We conclude this chapter by emphasizing that building an effective team goes beyond simply recruiting talented individuals. True leadership involves the ability to identify hidden potential, cultivate genuine diversity, manage interpersonal differences, empower with confidence, and continually invest in employee development. The inclusive, diverse, and empowering approach adopted by Jesus provides a timeless and inspiring model for modern leaders.

This chapter, enriched with contemporary examples and deep analyses of Jesus's leadership practices, aims to serve as a robust guide for CEOs and managers who wish to create strong, motivated, and resilient teams, prepared to face the complex and dynamic challenges of the future.

# Chapter 3

## Conflict Management

## Harmonizing Differences the Way Jesus Did

Conflict, an inevitable presence in human experience, can represent both the greatest challenge and the greatest opportunity for growth within any organization. Jesus, one of history's greatest transformational leaders, did not shy away from conflicts but addressed them directly with courage, wisdom, and profound compassion. His actions, filled with authenticity and coherence, taught timeless principles about resolution, reconciliation, and building lasting relationships. In this chapter, we delve deeper into how Jesus confronted these challenges and how his strategies can translate into effective modern management practices, especially in critical areas like transparent communication, genuine forgiveness, and proactive conflict resolution.

## Teachings on Forgiveness and Conflict Resolution

Forgiveness is not merely an abstract spiritual concept but a powerful and pragmatic tool for effectively managing conflicts. Jesus not only preached forgiveness but embodied it fully, exemplifying the importance of releasing grievances and rebuilding broken relationships. In contemporary corporate contexts, fostering a culture of forgiveness promotes healthier environments, where teams feel safe to innovate without fear of making mistakes. Companies like Pixar embody this philosophy, valuing continuous learning and viewing mistakes as opportunities to improve and grow collectively. By fostering an environment where forgiveness is valued, modern leaders not only solve conflicts but strengthen interpersonal bonds, boosting creativity and collaboration.

## Emphasis on Open Communication and Honesty

Jesus was a master of clear, direct, and deeply meaningful communication. By using parables and analogies, he translated complex truths into accessible and memorable messages. This style resonates strongly in modern management, where clarity and transparency are essential to maintaining trust within teams. Business leaders like Indra Nooyi, former CEO of PepsiCo, adopt this frank and honest approach, creating an organizational culture of openness, mutual trust, and ongoing dialogue. By encouraging honest communication, conflicts can be swiftly resolved before becoming harmful, creating a more harmonious and productive workplace.

## The Example of Washing Feet: Humility in Leadership

By washing the feet of his disciples, Jesus completely overturned traditional expectations about leadership and hierarchy. With this simple yet deeply symbolic gesture, he demonstrated that true leadership is based on humility, service to others, and the willingness to place collective needs above individual ones. This practice is embraced today by inspirational leaders like Ken Frazier, CEO of Merck, who emphasizes the importance of listening and learning from all organizational levels. This humble leadership style facilitates peaceful conflict resolution by creating an environment of mutual respect and genuine consideration, where everyone feels valued.

# Conflict Management with Empathy and Assertiveness

Jesus uniquely combined genuine empathy with clear assertiveness. He profoundly understood people's emotions and perspectives yet did not hesitate to act decisively when needed. This balance provides valuable lessons on emotional intelligence, empathy, and adaptability in modern leadership. Satya Nadella of Microsoft exemplifies this balance, where his empathetic approach paired with assertive decision-making has significantly transformed the company's culture, reducing conflicts and encouraging creative collaboration. Modern leaders who incorporate empathy with assertiveness can resolve conflicts constructively, preserving valuable relationships while maintaining strategic objectives.

# Jesus' Lessons on Managing Diverse Personalities

Conflicts are inevitable in any human group, and Jesus' team was no exception. Various biblical accounts document disagreements among his followers, whether regarding recognition, ideological differences, or communication failures. However, Jesus consistently promoted a culture of openness, dialogue, and forgiveness, demonstrating that conflicts are not insurmountable problems but opportunities for growth. Modern conflict resolution models, such as the one developed by Kenneth Thomas and Ralph Kilmann, emphasize the effectiveness of the empathetic and dialogical approach that Jesus employed, teaching business leaders how to create healthy environments where conflicts are positively managed and leveraged as drivers for organizational development.

## Lessons from Jesus on Continuous Development

Jesus continually invested in his team's development through teachings, reflections, and continuous feedback. He created an environment where disciples could continually learn and grow, which is essential in modern talent management practices. Companies like Microsoft, Google, and Amazon strongly emphasize continuous development and professional empowerment of their teams, offering ongoing learning opportunities, training, and regular feedback, practices that Jesus already employed in his daily leadership.

We conclude this chapter by reinforcing that building an effective team goes beyond merely recruiting talented individuals. True leadership involves identifying hidden potentials, cultivating genuine diversity, managing interpersonal differences, confidently empowering others, and continuously investing in growth.

By integrating historical principles with contemporary, proven management techniques, modern leaders can transform conflicts, typically seen as destructive, into valuable opportunities for relational strengthening, continuous learning, and organizational growth. Thus, conflicts become effective pathways for deepening mutual understanding, promoting sustainable growth, and creating collaborative organizational cultures. This chapter marks an essential part of a transformative journey, providing tools for CEOs and managers to face complex challenges effectively and dynamically.

# Chapter 4

## Empowerment and Delegation

## Jesus's Mastery in Trusting and Strengthening

The true test of leadership often lies beyond merely accomplishing tasks; it resides primarily in the ability to genuinely trust and empower others. Jesus demonstrated exceptional mastery in this aspect, perfectly balancing the delegation of responsibilities with the profound empowerment of his followers. He delegated tasks, but more importantly, he empowered people to grow, flourish, and assume responsibilities with confidence and purpose. This chapter explores how Jesus's extraordinary example of delegation and empowerment can enrich and transform contemporary corporate leadership practices, creating vibrant organizations and exceptional leaders.

## Delegation with Purpose: The Disciples' Missions

Delegation in Jesus's leadership was strategic and intentionally purposeful. By sending seventy disciples, two by two, to prepare his way, Jesus not only assigned tasks but genuinely fostered autonomy, personal growth, and practical learning. He demonstrated absolute confidence in their capabilities, creating significant developmental opportunities. In a modern context, leaders like Mary Barra, CEO of General Motors, adopt this same strategic approach, empowering internal leaders to make decisions aligned with the company's overall goals, promoting decentralized leadership that enhances agility, innovation, and engagement.

## Developing Leaders through Delegation

Jesus deeply understood that effective delegation is crucial for developing resilient and capable leaders. By sending Peter and John to organize the Last Supper, he entrusted them not merely with logistical responsibilities but deeply involved them in a symbolic and spiritually significant leadership experience. This approach mirrors the contemporary leadership philosophy practiced by Jack Welch at General Electric, who recognized the vital importance of delegation and mentorship in shaping future organizational leaders, continuously strengthening the company's internal capability and potential.

## Empowering Decision-Making

The ability to empower disciples to make independent decisions is powerfully illustrated when Jesus slept in the boat during a storm. His momentary apparent absence allowed disciples to confront and resolve problems themselves, promoting growth and self-confidence. This approach parallels practices of visionary leaders such as Sundar Pichai at Google, who emphasizes empowering teams to autonomously discover innovative solutions, building an environment of deep trust, limitless creativity, and continuous innovation.

## Consequences of Delegation: Facing Mistakes

Jesus fully understood that delegation implied risks, including errors and failures, exemplified in Peter's denial. However, he saw these failures not as moments of defeat but as precious opportunities for learning and growth. Similarly, Jeff Bezos at Amazon fosters a culture where failures are considered essential steps towards innovation and significant progress, encouraging teams to take risks, learn, and continually evolve.

# Problem Solving and Autonomy

Jesus frequently encouraged his disciples to think critically and independently solve problems. When confronted with the need to feed thousands of people, Jesus first asked his disciples how they would approach the challenge before intervening with the multiplication of loaves and fishes. This effective method stimulated autonomy, creativity, and initiative. Satya Nadella, CEO of Microsoft, implements similar principles by fostering an organizational culture centered on continuous growth, autonomous learning, and proactive problem-solving.

We conclude this chapter recognizing that empowerment and delegation are powerful, transformative tools, especially when applied with the wisdom and intentionality demonstrated by Jesus. Contemporary leaders can draw valuable inspiration from this model to create a robust, self-sustaining culture of leadership that encourages innovation, collective responsibility, and individual growth.

Delegation is not merely an operational necessity; it is a strategic opportunity to cultivate talent, strengthen interpersonal relationships, and prepare organizations to face future challenges with courage and confidence. The inspiring legacy left by Jesus provides a practical guide for implementing effective empowerment and delegation practices, illustrated by tangible and relevant examples from contemporary business leaders. By adopting these deeply human principles, modern leaders can not only drive exceptional results but also build resilient, adaptable, and deeply engaged teams capable of positively transforming their organizations and communities.

# Chapter 5

## Marketing Strategies

## Communicating Vision through Parables and Actions

Effective marketing isn't simply about promoting products or services; it's about conveying a powerful message that resonates deeply with the audience, inspiring authentic and lasting actions. Jesus Christ exemplified this mastery, using parables and symbolic actions that not only clearly communicated his vision but also touched people's hearts and minds. In this chapter, we will deeply explore how Jesus's unique and effective communication methods can be integrated into contemporary marketing strategies, emphasizing the vital importance of authenticity, emotional impact, and consistency in corporate messaging.

## Parables as Effective Communication Tools

Jesus was an exceptional communicator, capable of transforming complex concepts into engaging, memorable, and meaningful stories. His parables conveyed profound wisdom and, above all, created intense and lasting emotional connections with listeners. This narrative technique, full of symbolism and simplicity, is clearly observable in the strategies of today's most influential brands. Apple, for instance, transcends merely selling products by sharing narratives that encapsulate a desirable lifestyle and innovative philosophy. Through authentic storytelling, Apple creates not just customers but genuine brand enthusiasts and advocates, much like Jesus's parables inspired and mobilized crowds.

## The Multiplication of Loaves and Fishes and the Concept of 'Virality'

The miraculous multiplication of loaves and fishes performed by Jesus symbolizes the extraordinary power of a singular act to generate widespread attention and significant social impact. This event quickly became well-known, capturing imaginations and spreading Jesus's fame across vast regions. In modern contexts, this "viral" effect is precisely what companies seek in their marketing campaigns. Brands like Red Bull exemplify this perfectly through bold events and impactful campaigns that immediately attract global attention, generating viral enthusiasm and significantly strengthening brand recognition.

# Brand Building through Consistent Actions and Values

Jesus's ministry was profoundly characterized by absolute consistency between his actions and messages. He fully embodied the values he preached, building profound credibility, authenticity, and trust among his followers. This approach highlights the critical importance of consistency in contemporary brand identity building. Companies like Patagonia, which rigorously integrate sustainable practices into all their operations and communication strategies, clearly demonstrate how consistent authenticity greatly strengthens consumer trust and loyalty, creating a solid, lasting foundation for the brand.

# Relationship Marketing: The Personal Approach of Jesus

Jesus deeply understood the essential importance of personal relationships and strong, engaged community-building in effectively disseminating his message. This fundamental principle holds even greater significance in modern marketing, where personalized engagement and individual experiences are key to customer loyalty and passionate brand advocacy. Companies like

Zappos excel by placing exceptional customer service at the heart of their strategy, turning routine interactions into memorable experiences that generate true loyalty and emotional support for the brand.

## Use of Symbols and Symbolic Actions

Jesus's triumphant entry into Jerusalem on Palm Sunday and the Last Supper are clear examples of the strategic use of symbols and symbolic actions to convey powerful messages. These memorable acts communicated his vision vividly and powerfully. Similarly, modern brands utilize symbolism effectively. For instance, brands like Nike use inspiring figures and iconic symbolism, powerfully communicating their fundamental and aspirational values. These symbols become powerful visual and emotional representations of the brand's identity and purpose.

We conclude this chapter emphasizing that the innovative and profoundly authentic marketing strategies used by Jesus—impactful parables, striking symbolic actions, and consistent values—offer valuable inspiration for contemporary practices. Modern leaders can draw significant insights from this model to create marketing strategies that inspire and mobilize audiences in a lasting way.

This chapter aims to empower business leaders with innovative perspectives on genuinely inspiring and effective communication of their visions, using meaningful stories, striking symbols, and authentic actions that resonate deeply with their audiences. By adopting these effective practices, contemporary leaders can inspire and mobilize lasting engagement.

# Chapter 6

## Servant Leadership

### Jesus's Supreme Example of Humility

Servant leadership, an increasingly revered concept in the contemporary corporate world, finds its most powerful and inspiring expression in the figure of Jesus Christ. By radically challenging traditional power and hierarchy structures, Jesus established a new form of leadership centered on genuine service, humility, and caring for others in every decision and action. This chapter deeply analyzes how the servant leadership exemplified by Jesus is intimately connected to modern leadership theories and practices, and how these principles can positively transform organizational cultures, making them stronger, more humane, and empathetic.

### Washing the Disciples' Feet: Humility in Action

One of the most striking and revolutionary examples of Jesus's servant leadership was the symbolic and deeply meaningful act of washing his disciples' feet. By performing this task reserved for the humblest servants, Jesus demonstrated that true greatness in leadership lies in selfless service and authentic humility. This inspiring act deeply resonates with contemporary business leaders like Ken Chenault, former CEO of American Express, who consistently prioritized his team's needs and well-being, establishing an organizational culture rooted in mutual respect and genuine commitment. Through the practice of servant leadership, Chenault not only strengthened employee loyalty and engagement but also fostered a workplace environment that values personal and collective growth.

## Leading by Example and Serving Others

Jesus did not merely teach the concept of serving others; he intensely lived this philosophy in every aspect of his life, becoming the ultimate example of this principle. In a modern corporate environment, leading by example is crucial for creating authenticity, respect, and trust in interpersonal relationships. Howard Schultz, founder of Starbucks, adopted this model by providing substantial employee benefits, including free university education. His proactive approach centered on employee well-being created an organizational culture where each team member feels valued and motivated, directly reflecting in customer service quality and overall company performance.

## Empathy and Active Listening in Servant Leadership

Jesus's exceptional ability to form deep connections with people, actively listening and demonstrating genuine empathy, highlights the critical importance of these qualities in modern leadership. Empathy and active listening not only strengthen interpersonal relationships but are essential for understanding the needs and challenges faced by teams. Leaders like Microsoft's Satya Nadella exemplify the transformative power of these skills. Under Nadella's empathetic leadership, Microsoft transformed its organizational culture into a much more inclusive, innovative environment focused on human and professional development.

## Challenges of Servant Leadership

While servant leadership offers numerous transformative benefits, it also presents real and complex challenges. A primary challenge is balancing genuine commitment to serving and supporting teams with the necessity of maintaining clear and effective authority in critical decision-making. Indra Nooyi, CEO of PepsiCo, directly confronted these challenges by implementing innovative employee wellness and development policies while simultaneously maintaining the company's operational efficiency and global market competitiveness. Balancing authority with effective service is fundamental for servant leadership success, requiring continuous self-assessment and adaptation.

## Sustainability and Legacy through Servant Leadership

More than simply an ethical and empathetic approach, servant leadership represents a powerful and sustainable strategy for creating lasting organizations with significant positive legacies. Jesus's ministry resulted in a movement that spanned centuries, sustained by profound values and coherent actions. Similarly, Patagonia, under the leadership of Yvon Chouinard, demonstrates how genuinely servant-oriented leadership can integrate sustainable practices and an organizational culture based on service and purpose. Patagonia not only thrived financially but also earned profound global respect for its integrity and commitment to collective and environmental well-being.

We conclude this chapter recognizing that servant leadership, as taught and lived by Jesus, represents a powerful and profoundly transformative philosophy for contemporary organizations. By adopting principles of humility, authentic service, and genuine empathy, modern leaders can create strong, resilient, and highly committed organizational cultures. Consistent practice of servant leadership not only fosters a positive workplace environment but also establishes solid foundations for lasting success and a legacy transcending generations.

Business leaders are invited to embrace servant leadership not as a weakness or renunciation of power, but as an effective and deeply human strategy for uplifting their teams, strengthening interpersonal relationships, and fostering organizational innovation and excellence. Placing the needs and development of others first, exactly as Jesus did, is key to fully unleashing human potential and achieving truly transformational and inspiring leadership.

# Chapter 7

## Crisis Management

## Jesus's Calmness and Insight in Times of Adversity

In moments of crisis, the true essence of leadership clearly emerges, revealing inner strength, serenity, and the unwavering ability to act purposefully. Throughout history, Jesus Christ demonstrated these qualities extraordinarily, confronting extreme challenges with a serenity transcending adverse circumstances, offering not only immediate solutions but profound lessons that stand the test of time. This chapter explores in detail how the strategies adopted by Jesus in managing severe crises can illuminate paths for contemporary business leaders, providing valuable insights for navigating difficulties with genuine compassion, strategic clarity, and inspiring conviction.

## Calm Amid the Storm

One of the most remarkable stories of Jesus's calm leadership is when he stilled a violent storm, bringing tranquility amidst chaos. This episode profoundly symbolizes the essence of true leadership in difficult times: maintaining calmness and demonstrating a confidence that inspires safety and stability in others. In the modern business world, leaders like Warren Buffett, known for his calm and rational approach during economic crises, embody this trait. Buffett has become a safe haven for worried investors, providing clear and reassuring guidance through thoughtful communications and balanced decisions, resulting in continuous business protection and growth even amid global financial turbulence.

## Preparation and Vigilance Against Complacency

The parable of the ten virgins strongly highlights the critical importance of constant preparedness and vigilance in the face of future uncertainty. Jesus taught that those who remain prepared are better equipped to face sudden and inevitable challenges. In a business context, this mindset is vital for effective leadership. Sundar Pichai, CEO of Google, exemplified this principle perfectly during the global pandemic, proactively anticipating necessary changes and preparing his company for the transition to remote work before it became mandatory. This approach allowed Google to remain efficient, productive, and united during one of the greatest crises of our generation, illustrating the importance of strategic vigilance and organizational adaptability.

## Cleansing the Temple: Decisive Action Facing Problems

Jesus's decisive action in driving merchants from the temple exemplifies the urgent necessity of directly confronting systemic issues and acting decisively to protect core values. Such clarity of decisive action is essential in modern leadership, particularly when facing deep systemic issues requiring firm and immediate interventions. Rosalind Brewer, CEO of Walgreens, embodies this attitude by addressing complex and sensitive issues related to racial equality, implementing clear, consistent, and visible measures to enhance diversity and inclusion within her company, demonstrating that decisive leadership can redefine organizational culture and reinforce ethical and moral principles.

# Mission-Focused in the Face of Danger

Jesus's unwavering determination while facing his inevitable destiny in Jerusalem provides a powerful lesson on the value of absolute commitment to the mission, even amidst imminent danger. The ability to remain faithful to the mission, regardless of external circumstances, is essential for effective crisis leadership. CEOs such as Ursula Burns of Xerox demonstrated this commitment by maintaining a clear and consistent vision during difficult restructuring periods and competitive challenges, ensuring their teams remained aligned with core objectives, reinforcing organizational purpose even under intense pressure.

# Communicating Purposefully During Crises

Even in the most challenging moments, Jesus's communication remained clear, firm, and deeply comforting. His words guided, offered comfort, and provided clarity in critical times, offering direction and hope even amid adversity. In today's corporate environment, leaders like Arne Sorenson, former CEO of Marriott International, adopted this same transparent and honest approach during crises, such as the COVID-19 pandemic, delivering direct and comforting messages that strengthened employee and stakeholder trust. The ability to communicate purposefully and transparently is essential to effectively managing crises and preserving organizational integrity and cohesion.

## Building Organizational Resilience for the Future

Jesus's approach to crises combined not only calmness and serenity but also deep compassion and strategic action clearly guided by his broader mission. This approach not only solved immediate problems but prepared his followers for future adversities, strengthening personal and collective resilience. Business leaders adopting this perspective not only address immediate crises but also create more robust and resilient organizations capable of confidently facing future challenges. By cultivating a culture of compassion, clarity, and conviction, they transform crises into opportunities for significant growth and lasting organizational strength.

We conclude this chapter recognizing that Jesus's unique approach to crisis management provides an exceptionally powerful model for contemporary leaders. His extraordinary ability to maintain serenity, make effective decisions, and communicate clearly even under great pressure not only resolved historical crises but created a lasting legacy of inspiration and resilience. Today's business leaders can find inspiration in these valuable lessons, using crises as opportunities to reaffirm their core mission, reinforce foundational values, and cultivate lasting trust and loyalty among their teams and stakeholders.

By integrating these timeless lessons into their leadership practices, managers can transform seemingly insurmountable challenges into significant growth opportunities, inspiring deep trust and building a solid and enduring foundation for their organizations and communities. Ultimately, effective crisis management, as exemplified by Jesus, is not merely about momentary survival but a unique opportunity to strengthen essential values and create a truly inspiring legacy.

# Chapter 8

## Innovation and Change

## Jesus's Revolutionary Model for Organizational Transformation

True innovation and the ability to effectively implement change require courage, vision, and the skill to comfortably challenge the status quo. The life and leadership of Jesus Christ exemplify these attributes perfectly, as he continually challenged established norms, introduced new perspectives, and promoted profound, lasting transformations. This chapter offers a detailed and inspiring analysis of how Jesus's innovative and courageous approach can serve as a revolutionary model for contemporary leaders seeking to cultivate innovation and drive meaningful changes within their organizations.

## Challenging Conventional Wisdom

Jesus frequently and openly questioned the cultural and religious norms of his time, encouraging people to think critically about deeply rooted values and traditions. He did not hesitate to defy social expectations, offering revolutionary interpretations of justice, mercy, and equality. This courageous spirit is also found in contemporary business leaders like Steve Jobs, founder of Apple, who completely revolutionized the technology world by challenging the conventional approach to creating and consuming digital products. By boldly confronting internal and external resistance, Jobs transformed how we interact with technology, creating a lasting legacy that redefined an entire industry.

## Establishing a New 'Organizational Culture'

Jesus introduced a new cultural approach grounded in principles of love, compassion, and inclusion. His message was clear: the true value of a community lies in equality and mutual care. Similarly, Kim Jordan, CEO of New Belgium Brewing, built a corporate culture grounded in sustainability, environmental respect, and social responsibility. Under her visionary leadership, the company became not only profitable but also a global reference for ethical business practices. This cultural transformation, like the one introduced by Jesus, emphasizes the importance of aligning daily actions with core values that inspire pride, commitment, and deep engagement among all members of the organization.

# Embracing Change and Promoting Adaptation

Jesus deeply understood that change was inevitable and necessary for spiritual and community growth. He continually prepared his followers to accept and embrace change, even when it required significant personal sacrifices. In modern times, visionary leaders like Sundar Pichai, CEO of Google, have demonstrated similar capabilities, proactively anticipating changes and preparing their organizations for rapid adaptation, as evidenced by Google's agile and effective response to the global pandemic, ensuring continuity and productivity through a smooth transition to remote work and virtualization of business processes.

# Challenging Conventional Wisdom

Through impactful parables and teachings, Jesus often encouraged his listeners to challenge their own assumptions and think beyond traditional limitations. He used simple yet profound metaphors that contained powerful truths capable of altering perspectives and inspiring new actions. Contemporary companies, such as Tesla under Elon Musk's visionary leadership, adopt similar approaches by radically challenging established conventions in the automotive and energy industries. By launching highly desirable electric vehicles and sustainable energy solutions, Tesla has not only transformed public perception of mobility but also accelerated innovation and redefined the global vehicle market.

## Mission Focus Amidst Danger

Jesus demonstrated unparalleled determination and absolute focus on his mission, even when facing extreme threats and adversity. His resolute journey toward Jerusalem, where he knew he would face death, symbolizes unwavering commitment to his principles and ultimate goals. Likewise, business leaders like Ursula Burns, former CEO of Xerox, demonstrate how maintaining a clear vision and determined focus during crises and market challenges ensures that organizations remain aligned and resilient, even in difficult times.

## Clear and Purposeful Communication

In crisis situations, Jesus's ability to communicate with clarity and profound meaning stood out. He did not simply convey information; his words provided hope, comfort, and clear direction. Effective business leaders, such as the late Arne Sorenson, CEO of Marriott during the COVID-19 crisis, demonstrated that honest, transparent, and intentional communication could inspire confidence, solidarity, and resilience across the organization, strengthening cohesion and enabling quicker and stronger recovery after the crisis period.

## Transforming Adversity into Opportunities

We conclude this chapter by emphasizing that following Jesus's example in times of crisis offers contemporary leaders a robust and inspiring model for transforming adversity into real opportunities for growth and innovation. The ability to face challenges with calmness, clear purpose, and decisive action not only resolves immediate issues but also strengthens the organization and its followers for the future. By cultivating organizational resilience and maintaining constant focus on the mission, contemporary leaders can ensure a sustainable legacy of success and inspire lasting trust and loyalty, making their organizations living examples of humanity's capacity to overcome adversity with courage, compassion, and continuous innovation.

This chapter demonstrates that following the exemplary principles of Jesus in crisis management allows leaders not only to confront adversity but also to thrive through it, creating robust and enduring organizations that leave inspiring legacies for future generations.

# Chapter 9

## Sustainability and Legacy

## Cultivating Lasting Growth and Influence with Jesus

Sustainability and legacy are more than modern corporate concepts; they are fundamental pillars defining leaders who aim to positively impact future generations. Jesus Christ is history's most powerful example of this truth. His leadership was neither momentary nor superficial; it was deeply strategic, aimed at cultivating enduring growth and influence transcending centuries and cultures. This chapter closely examines how Jesus built a sustainable legacy through his actions, teachings, and influence, providing an inspiring and practical guide for contemporary business leaders seeking to create organizations and cultures that endure beyond their tenure.

## Planting Seeds for Long-Term Growth

Through parables like the sower, Jesus taught the importance of patience, long-term vision, and ongoing investment in fundamental values that yield sustainable results over time. He emphasized that not all seeds produce fruit immediately, but those planted in fertile soil inevitably yield abundant results. In modern business contexts, this lesson is evident in strategies adopted by companies such as Amazon, led by Jeff Bezos, consistently prioritizing long-term investments in innovation and infrastructure over immediate profits, ensuring robust, continuous growth for decades.

## Building Communities and the Power of Networks

Jesus didn't simply convey individual teachings; he built a strong, committed network of followers who ensured his message endured long after his earthly life. This ability to create committed, self-sustaining communities is a critical aspect of lasting leadership. Business leaders, such as Ray Anderson, founder of Interface Inc., employed this principle by transforming their companies into pioneering sustainability models, building conscious business communities that inspired an entire industry to rethink its practices. Anderson created not only a legacy within his own organization but also extended his influence beyond corporate boundaries, promoting profound and systemic change.

## Developing Leaders for Sustainability

Jesus devoted significant time to developing and empowering leaders who could continue his mission after his departure. He personally invested in his disciples, preparing them to assume responsibilities and spread his message worldwide. This critical practice is clearly visible in business leaders like Jack Welch of General Electric, who dedicated substantial attention to mentoring and developing internal leaders, ensuring his organization's strength and direction even after his retirement. This transformational leadership model, inspired by Jesus's practice, significantly strengthens organizations by ensuring continuity of vision and organizational commitment.

## Encouraging Continuous Innovation

Jesus constantly challenged his followers to think beyond traditional conventions, encouraging them to explore new ways of thinking and acting that would allow his message to thrive across diverse cultures and eras. This spirit of constant innovation is vividly reflected in modern companies like Google, initially led by Larry Page and Sergey Brin, where continuous innovation and constant questioning of the status quo are core corporate values. By encouraging continuous experimentation and adaptation, these companies remain relevant and dynamic, always prepared to address new challenges and opportunities.

## Persisting Through Adversity

Jesus's resilience in the face of adversity is particularly inspiring. He remained steadfast in his vision and purpose, even amidst fierce criticism, persecution, and extreme hardship. This principle is mirrored by business leaders like Elon Musk, who, despite criticisms, financial challenges, and significant regulatory barriers, steadfastly pursued his revolutionary vision for electric transportation and space exploration. These leaders' resilience and determination highlight the critical importance of persistence in adversity to create lasting influence and a meaningful legacy.

## Communicating with Clarity and Conviction

Jesus's exceptional ability to communicate clearly, especially during crises and adversity, allowed him to guide and strengthen those around him, solidifying his lasting influence.

Modern leaders who adopt transparent, authentic communication, like the late Arne Sorenson, former CEO of Marriott, who navigated the COVID-19 crisis with clear, empathetic messages, reinforce their credibility and build stakeholder trust. Effective crisis communication, inspired by Jesus's example, establishes a solid foundation of trust and loyalty, essential for sustainable success.

This chapter concludes with a powerful reflection on how legacy and sustainability are intertwined with a leader's ability to inspire and cultivate lasting growth. Jesus's example provides contemporary leaders with a clear, inspiring vision for creating organizations that not only endure the test of time but continually thrive. By adopting principles of patient investment, leadership development, continuous innovation, effective communication, and resilience, today's leaders can leave a profound, positive organizational legacy impacting future generations.

True transformational leadership isn't confined to immediate success; it plants seeds that flourish well beyond direct management. By following Jesus's example, business leaders can ensure their organizations are effective and successful today while being prepared to create a positive, inspiring impact on the world for generations to come.

# Conclusion

## "Jesus Christ: The Greatest CEO of All Time"

As we conclude our exploration of the life and teachings of Jesus Christ through the lens of management and business leadership, it is clear that the principles He exemplified transcend barriers of time, culture, and religion. The wisdom of Jesus, when applied to the business world, offers a revolutionary approach capable of transforming not only individuals and organizations but society as a whole.

Jesus, as the archetype of the ultimate leader, demonstrated a clear vision, an unparalleled ability to build and maintain a diverse team, the skill to manage conflicts with empathy, and a strategy to communicate a message that resonated and endured. His servant leadership established a paradigm for empowerment and delegation, encouraged innovation and change, and promoted sustainability and a lasting legacy.

In this book, we have explored how business leaders can adopt Jesus's wisdom to cultivate strong teams, confidently face crises, and inspire innovation and change. We have seen how Jesus's emphasis on building genuine relationships, serving others, and maintaining a coherent vision can inform leadership practices in any context.

The conclusion is clear: by following Jesus's example, leaders can achieve more than material success; they can cultivate a sense of purpose, community, and well-being that benefits everyone. Jesus's leadership lessons serve as a guide for creating an impact that is not only immediate but resonates across generations, building companies that are sustainable, resilient, and truly serve society.

Reflecting on "Jesus Christ: The Greatest CEO of All Time," we are invited to consider not only our effectiveness as leaders but also the legacy we wish to leave behind. Leadership inspired by Jesus goes beyond metrics and profit margins to touch the heart of human experience, inviting us to lead with compassion, vision, and an unwavering commitment to values that uplift and enrich everyone involved.

This book is not merely a comparison between two worlds; it is an invitation to reflect on the power of transformational leadership and how it can be applied to create a better future for leaders, followers, and communities around the world.

# Appendix

## Tools for Reflection and Leadership Development

This appendix is designed as a resource for leaders and study groups wishing to delve deeper into the concepts discussed in this book. It contains a series of tools aimed at facilitating personal reflection, leadership growth, and deeper understanding. Leaders and teams can use these resources to cultivate thoughtful discussions, enhance their leadership skills, and practically apply the leadership lessons presented.

# Reflection and Leadership Development Tools

### 1. Self-Assessment:

• How do you define leadership success?

• Which leadership qualities exemplified by Jesus do you recognize in yourself, and which ones do you wish to develop further?

### 2. Planning and Goal Setting:

• How clearly are your personal and organizational goals communicated?

• What steps will you take to integrate Jesus's leadership principles into your personal and organizational objectives?

## 3. Team Building:

• Evaluate the diversity of your team and discuss how it contributes to innovation and different viewpoints.

• What methods does your organization use to manage diverse personalities and resolve conflicts effectively?

## 4. Crisis Management:

• What valuable lessons has your organization learned from past crises?

• How can leadership improve communication during times of crisis?

## 5. Marketing Strategies:

• What narratives does your organization use to create meaningful connections with customers?

• How can your organization better use storytelling and symbolic actions to reinforce brand values?

6. Innovation and Change:

• How does your organization encourage and support innovation?

• What changes can you implement to further encourage innovation and adaptability?

7. Team Building:

• Discuss instances when delegation was effective in your organization, and identify areas for improvement.

• How do you balance the need for control with trust in your team?

8. Servant Leadership:

• In what ways can servant leadership principles be better integrated into your leadership style?

• How can your organization foster a culture of humility and authentic service?

9. Sustainability and Legacy:

• How does your organization ensure sustainability and long-term impact?

• How can you cultivate a culture focused on sustainability, responsibility, and positive legacy?

# Personal Reflection and Leadership Development Questions

## 1. Vision and Mission:

• How clearly does your organization communicate its mission to employees and clients?

• In what ways can you strengthen alignment between personal, organizational, and community values?

## 2. Planning and Goals:

• What specific objectives can you set to become a more effective and transformational leader?

• How will you measure progress toward achieving these goals?

3. Skill Development:

• What specific skills do you need to develop to enhance your leadership capabilities?

• Which resources or training programs would help you advance these skills effectively?

4. Mentorship and Team Growth:

• How can you actively mentor and develop team members to grow their leadership potential?

• What mentorship strategies can you implement to foster strong leadership within your organization?

This appendix is designed to be a practical resource for personal and organizational growth, empowering leaders and teams to implement the leadership lessons inspired by Jesus Christ. The intention is that these reflective exercises and questions will foster continuous development, resulting in positive and meaningful transformations within organizations and communities.